A
Pacific Northwest
Publisher

Copyright © 2012 by Keith Moul

All rights reserved. No part of this book may be reproduced or transmitted in any form by any means, electronic or mechanical, including photocopying and recording, without the prior written permission of the publishers, except by a reviewer who may quote brief passages in a review to be printed in a newspaper, magazine, or journal.

ISBN-10: 0985902809

ISBN-13: 978-0-9859028-0-3

Published by Broken Publications.
www.brokenpublications.com

Cover Image by Keith Moul

Cover layout: Jennifer-Crystal Johnson
www.jennifercrystaljohnson.com

Edited by Jennifer-Crystal Johnson

For more about Keith Moul, please e-mail: moulpoemsphotos@gmail.com.

With contributions by Ianthe Moul. For more on this artist, visit: www.iantheart.com

RECONSIDERED LIGHT
(With Contributions by Ianthe Moul)

By

Keith Moul

ACKNOWLEDGMENTS

POEMS WITH PHOTOS

Analectic Literary Magazine, "Red Barn, Northeast Washington," Vol.1, #1, July 31, 2011, np.
donotlookatthesun, "Few Cars," Iceland, 377, Long Road from Husavik, Issue 5, Postcards from Paris, Spring, 2011, np.
Porchlight, "Lily Pads," WA 1, Issue #5, Summer, 2010, p.51.
Puffin Circus, "Ireland, 1992," Ireland, 6, Volume 1, Issue 4, 2010, p.7.
Status Hat, "Spokane Tree, 1986", WA 5-1, October, 2010, np; "Skagit River, Below Diablo Dam, WA SR 20, Skagit River, #14-1," October, 2010, np.

POEMS ALONE

Bareback, "Buda, for or Against, Pest," June, 2012, np.
Cartier Street Review, "The Man on the Bremerton Ferry," June, 2012, pp 7-10.

PHOTOS ALONE

Bareback, "Lock, Series 5560," Portland, #112-1, April, 2012, np.
Centrifugal Eye, "Bridge Unsafe, Cross at Own Risk," Volume 5, Issue 3, August, 2010, p.64.
Diverse Voices Quarterly, "WA SR 20, North Cascades National Park, #147," Volume 3, Issue 8, 2011, cover.
Jerseyworks, "WA Palouse 23, Steptoe Butte 323, High on Steptoe Butte, Fall, 2011, np.
Ken*Again, "Mount Rainer National Park #336," Volume 11, No.3, Fall, 2010, np; "WA 208-2 Whatcom County, expected September, 2012.
Stirring, "Missouri, Jefferson City Capitol Building, #479-1," Volume 14, Editions 3-4, March/April, 2012, cover.
Straight Forward, "WA Palouse 13 #301-1, Generational Ties on the Palouse," 6/3/12, cover and p.21.

The Writing Disorder, "OR Central, Abandoned House #181, Blue Effulgence 2," expected Fall, 2012; "Or Central, Abandoned House #184, Blue Effulgence 1," expected Fall, 2012.
Vanilla, "WA SR 20, Too Long Out of Water #91, Neighbors Passed," Issue 6, 2-22-11, np.

PHOTOS OF PAINTINGS BY IANTHE MOUL

Verdad, "Nest of Anenomes," Volume 10, Spring, 2011, np; "The Elusive Purple Cow," Volume 10, Spring, 2011, np.

TABLE OF CONTENTS

IANTHE

Photo: Portrait of the Artist as a Young Girl	12
Portrait of the Artist as a Young Girl	13
Photo: The Elusive Purple Cow (painting)	14
The Elusive Purple Cow	15
Photo: Dory in Shady Cove (painting)	16
Taking the Cat, Gladly	17
Photo: Nest of Anenomes (painting)	18
Ontology in a Nest of Anemones	19

EARLIER

Photo: At Bruges, Belgium	22
At Bruges, Belgium	23
Photo: At the Rodin Museum, Paris	24
At the Rodin Museum, Paris	25
Photo: Bridge Unsafe, Cross at Own Risk 1	26
Photo: Bridge Unsafe, Cross at Own Risk 2	26
Bridge Unsafe, Cross at Own Risk	27
Photo: "Ciao Ricky"	28
"Ciao Ricky" Sidewalk Greeting, Milan, 1985	29
Photo: Coastal Fog, Oregon	30
Coastal Fog, Oregon	31
Photo: Eye of the Tree, at Dungeness Spit	32
Eye of the Tree, at Dungeness Spit	33
Photo: Ireland	34
Ireland	35
Photo: Iron Oxide, My Chance at Peace	36
Iron Oxide, My Chance at Peace	37
Photo: Lewis River, Lower Falls	38
Lewis River, Lower Falls	39
Photo: Lily Pads	40
Lily Pads	41
Photo: North Plains, Oregon	42
North Plains, Oregon	43
Photo: Notre Dame Cathedral, Paris	44

Notre Dame Cathedral, Paris 45
    Photo: Portuguese Wave 46
Portuguese Wave 47
    Photo: Red Barn, Northeast Washington 48
Red Barn, Northeast Washington 49
    Photo: Round Sky with Clouds 50
Round Sky with Clouds 51
    Photo: Skagit River, Below Diablo Dam 52
Skagit River, Below Diablo Dam 53
    Photo: Spokane Tree 54
Spokane Tree 55
    Photo: Waiting for Secrets 56
Waiting for Secrets 57

LATER

    Photo: Amelia at Pacific City, Oregon 1 60
Amelia at Pacific City, Oregon 1 61
    Photo: Amelia at Pacific City, Oregon 2 62
Amelia at Pacific City, Oregon 2 63
    Photo: Blue Effulgence 1 64
Blue Effulgence 1 65
    Photo: Blue Effulgence 2 66
Blue Effulgence 2 67
    Photo: Buda, For or Against, Pest 68
Buda – For or Against – Pest, 2007 69
    Photo: Capitol Building, Jefferson City 70
Capitol Building, Jefferson City 71
    Photo: Few Cars 72
Few Cars 73
    Photo: Generational Ties on the Palouse 74
Generational Ties on the Palouse 75
    Photo: High on Steptoe Butte 76
High on Steptoe Butte 77
    Photo: Lock, Series 5560 78
Lock, Series 5560 79
    Photo: Mount Rainier 80
Mount Rainier 81
    Photo: Neighbors Passed 82

Neighbors Passed	83
Photo: New Light's Hard Bargain	84
New Light's Hard Bargain	85
Photo: Nor Iron, Nor Rock, Nor Gold	86
Nor Iron, Nor Rock, Nor Gold	87
Photo: Orange Fog in Pursuit Up H Street	88
Orange Fog in Pursuit Up H Street	89
Photo: Spite the Obvious	90
Spite the Obvious	91
Photo: The Man on the Bremerton Ferry	92
The Man on the Bremerton Ferry	93
Photo: Washington State Route 20	96
Washington State Route 20	97
Photo: Crater Without Device	98
Crater Without Device	99
Photo: No Argument Rises	100
No Argument Rises	101

IANTHE

Portrait of the Artist as a Young Girl

My photo found you
receiving succor in light
and shade, a lucky moment
for us both. Your nature
let the scene surround you
and concentrate its force
in promise and resolve.

From the trees I watched
the filtered light
at a perfect angle
stipple hallowed ground,
prompt my shutter
to release this image
that now, with each encounter,
enriches my concentrated memory
and engenders my surprise.

Since then you have found your way,
always in light, always alert
to objects that light enhances.
In acrylic you tend your garden,
you bend erotic shapes, you
work to perfect a lip
edging toward a smile.

The Elusive Purple Cow

One day you were my girl,
vivacious in a river of soul,
friendly among diverse minds,
accepting of spirits whirling
toward you, or whirling away.

But then you snuck up on me
and favored me with surprise:
your artist eyes focused on light,
your color-voice shaking leaves
and placing gold at the feet
of a luminous, purple cow,
calm in its element and ministerial.

I turn back to my photos of you through the years
that (now gracing our walls and better nooks)
present my parent's elemental pride:
here in numerous forests, there
at many falls, so often at the nearby ocean
where your photogenic face captured mystery
and, presumably, stored it for your future use.

Lately we've talked in confident voices
of how, as artist, you choose your subjects,
render them distinct, caught in nature's tints,
wholly composed to your satisfaction. In all
your efforts, I hope you let me be with you.

Taking the Cat, Gladly

If, like you, I could row
to shade to rest from the sun,
past sharp bends upriver
and beach my craft
in a cool spot, I would.

Your arms welcome the effort;
your forehead beads sweat; you kneel
on sand, home, utter your prayer
of thanks to the cove for this return.

If, from over your shoulder, I
who see but do not feel
the mystery that you honor,
could help you recreate the scene
as reverence to living text, I would.

You know only what you know,
you alter only the prism
that splits hot light
into your spectral vision.

In your studio back home
dusk comes on, your cat,
Domingo, settles on your lap.
As heat within you rises, if
I may I gladly take your cat;
while you pour forth your sun
from molten light
within you.

Ontology in a Nest of Anemones

Any color omitted subtracts being from the whole:
remove dominant pink and tiny fish dine elsewhere;
mute the green and glycerol formed by algae dissipates;
cover the yellow eye and shrimp live lives very differently;
break this cycle and the sea reconfigures orderly death.

I hope to see the rainbow and learn to avoid the sting;
I am fully satisfied to swim in glory among the living;
I will go cautiously, with the tugging current, and dive
To bear true witness to this ever-turbulent kaleidoscope.

EARLIER

At Bruges, Belgium

When connected to the sea, Bruges flourished.
The sea receded by fifty miles. The most holy
saw evil in citizens' hearts. But Bruges elders
painted its gables in nostalgic colors, dredged
its canals, encouraged more bright Flemish cloth,
and lectured their offspring toward repentance.

So, accustomed daily to the stoop of it,
a woman sweeps each stair to the water,
easily outlasting many manufactured brooms.

Then, with much the same mind, she shines
her windows, virtue at the family sills
compelling her to clean her way to approval.

I drift on by, but turn to know the soul of it,
her red linen apron, her duty, her function
to start at the top, as had her mothers,
to follow her line into immortality
through the up, down, and passing by of lives.

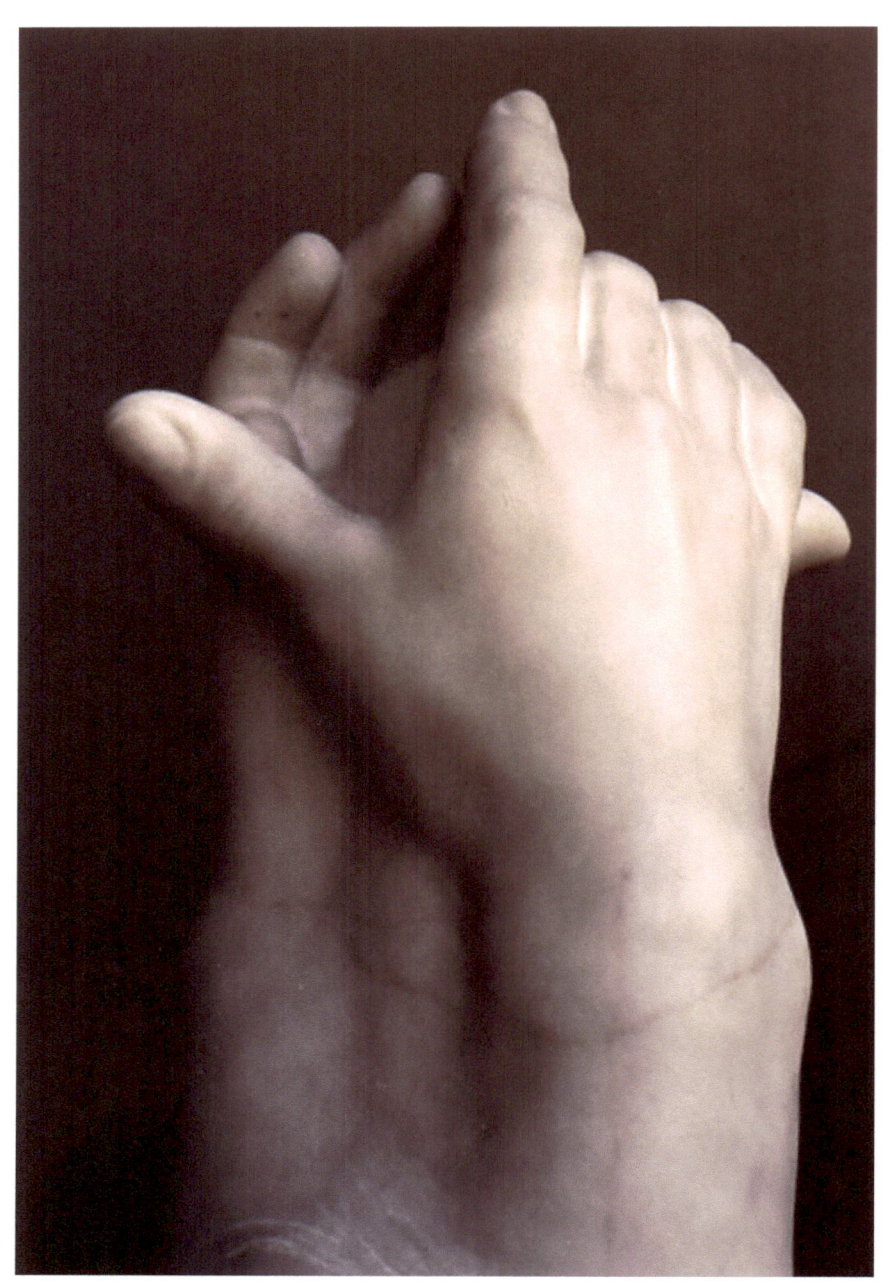

At the Rodin Museum, Paris

At the gateway, in the courtyard,
throughout the building and grounds,
I am drawn by the hands, their size,
their power, their subtlety in bronze.

Each hand needs extra space to occupy:
where it tests its freedom of form,
where it proves itself worthy
of its freedom of touch, enfolding both
what it needs and what it wants.

Available to each hand is the unseen,
that which will be next to be caressed,
wrung, or shaken until its object knows
the same purpose of its space as the hand;
or the hand's pair waits, ready nearby,
as resolute, gentle, or steady as required;
each alone fixes the other exponentially.

I cannot contain the space of these hands.
I may as well bottle the air that fills
the space, or fend the light, or fight
the dark that naturally surrounds them.

Rodin's hands sculpted their space,
added each fitting medium to make them firm,
then let his fingers, stone or bronze,
point out some meaning at the gate, up
the lane, hulking from squalid apartments; or
let me sit nearby, deep in thought
for as long as it takes, or
until the gateman ushers me out.

Bridge Unsafe: Cross at Own Risk

Over generations, humor blackens in its wait for new blood;
those singing laughs exited the back door of the bar at LaPush
while nasal sniggers erupt when any pass by the old slough bridge.

The tide twice every day rolls in, then leaks away past rigid pilings,
with each moon cracking planks, as madness in visual display.
Gulls land here seldom, birds too risk averse, even to crack a crab;
fish flee creosote ooze that glosses everything with afternoon shine.

Will weather bluster in to change this work of carpenters' hands?
Was it only 50 years when the last pick-up, once over, feared return?

Can a photographer of arid mind claim any of this is worth a laugh?

"Ciao, Ricky," Sidewalk Greeting, Milan, 1985

For years since, I have always remembered
this sidewalk hello with flowers and chalk
meant for all passersby along with absent Ricky.
Graffiti, all right, but this is light Italian dessert,
endearing with more than a handful of absurdity.

My poem occurs now as a form of apology,
after too many indulgences, for all the Rickys
to whom I lent no time, all the lonely sidewalks
forming countless lonely corners to lonely blocks.

Whether flowers in a vase have helped I do not know.
Flowers can be had at little cost, but chalk at hand
betokens thoughtfulness and an original nature, or
an artist, or a child, or a moonlighting gangster
ensnared in contradictions, working streets in private.
But I think no one brings chalk to a street fight.

Perhaps what I see has more to do with national character
than personal warmth, more the Italian unselfconsciousness
from lovemaking among ruins, shards of pigment discarded
among ancient pastels, hot sun browning hills, scorching air.
Perhaps vivacious greeting, taken away whole, can endure.

Coastal Fog, Oregon

In the coastal forest, one tree anchors fog down low,
trickling from branches: an ordinary enough tree day,
here.
        As I begin my walk toward the land's edge,
I smell the sea's edge, ripe with the sea's jetsam;
I hear the gulls' sharp report of hunger; I bathe
in the air's wet alliance with the sea; it staggers me.

Along the path, I have forgotten details of yesterday;
I step into the spongy resting place of a fallen cedar;
there are no echoes here, but I feel common surrender,
late in creation's timetable, a furor of living and dying
beneath so many surfaces, just below my feet, out of reach.

Were my bones less complicitous, the fog might stop me cold.

Eye of the Tree at Dungeness Spit

When the great tree fell,
not all at once, but
like a loved horse dying of hunger,
the living tree strength failed
as decay gnawed it inside. Those still
living nearby remembered
until they went their ways
and the summer birds returned.

Later, the tree migrated here
as swells took hold of it, depositing
it on the long strand of monotone tides,
among tree bones hinting of forests.

Seabirds search crackling stones
and escape the sucking undertow,
content with bits of flesh expelled
as from a stinking maw near the scoured tree
and altering universes of sand.

Through this glass,
children of the present move
toward, then away from
the beached altar, laughing
paeans at its scars, ignorant
of its physical past, certain
of their luck with coincidence.

Ireland
(Powers Court)

A white horse
wandered into this light,
bowed to the grass's pull
a moment before a gallop.

Many forces stir
beneath a sultry peace
(this is the Republic!),
suitable for framing.

Battle scars lie buried
behind eyes, in the sharp
wit and loud voices
ringing at the pubs.

Had I talent for song,
I would sing here, in shade
beneath the ancient green hills,
with shining gardens at my back.

Iron Oxide, My Chance at Peace
(Hillsboro, OR)

Morning sun layers with more rust a neglected fence post;
ignored all fall, dry, tall grasses wave in sleeves of ice;
beyond these, vision blurs in space surplus to the image:
so far, no world-shards pierce this favored sac of light,
nor is their exclusion explained by other than my chance.

I took my chance at peace, an early walk, near my new home.

Not that all incendiary change is bad: imagine a universe
void of fire rocks, world series, and insect metamorphosis.
Or, think of creation's soup, set a-boil, not yet fulfilled,
not yet fueling the beat, pumping passion's ejaculation.

So, the face conceals the body's chemistry in its quiet guise;
the blood courses with quiet and regular pulse, its own stream;
the brain contains its quiet sparks, mostly private fireworks;
all certain in the silent morning sending signals through the rust.

Lewis River, Lower Falls

That such undiscovered treasures still exist
comes as no surprise: we have not seen it all,
with dog-days coming on. We like erasures
of our ignorance, especially high, cool, and total.

You had been happy on our small plot, puttering
among your speckled lilies, awaiting discoveries.
I had appeared in several long lines, waiting my turn.
Neither had warned the other of impending change.

Then intuition got the better of complacency.
Character stepped forward. Cunning of a kind
revealed advantages to be had at higher altitude,
short of flight. We were moved to circle, then back.

Heading upward toward the source of steady water
cannot, for sanity, become an everyday event:
we must feel close to each other, close to forever,
close to the rush of purity, composed in light,

close to crystal intelligence, anxious with desire.

After the falls, Eve, the titillation, the cedars, the moss,
and pleasure filled me to aver my adamant Adamness,
hot, hard, and bent on revelation on the quiet forest lap.

Lily Pads

Uncommon quiet, beside freeways, in a large city,
on a walk through its arboretum at the lake's edge,
I find ways through light to the surface of depths.

Regularly hard light enters at this angle its spectrum;
I position myself, not for mystery, but natural law
continuing to summon me to its litigations.

Spectral bubbles offer themselves in evidence – sustained!
Fins flash survival, scales feed on flakes of sun – sustained!
Lily pads, your argument in this light is clear and convincing!

The medium, fresh water serves as venue and arbiter, too:
wise in its ways, unswayed by irrelevance or immateriality,
the lake binds the day's light into justice, freed or imprisoned.

On oblique images caught in amber I can only muse. What
of forgotten worlds? What of future implications? What
of incongruities of shadows, uncertainties of nether light?

I will not wait and measure dark's effect. I will not wait
to quibble over change or babble on about lost opportunities.
I will weigh all facts, determine fair sentence, then hand it down.

North Plains, Oregon

My recent move provides me new terrain; I wander
renaming space as what I know to be unexplored place.
It may be my only way. Early winter numbs my brain,
but still I flush concealed colors ripe for picking.

So my first claim is made, the photo of discovery,
a small memento of conquest, a so long to what I had.
Winter helped, sneaking in last night without an ounce
of sentiment, spiking pegs to hoist its evangelical tent.

So far, native fauna eludes my lens. After all, territory
costs a serious price, including many hidden, even
subterranean rights. I store away my berries
for more welcoming days, more forgiving nights.

Notre Dame Cathedral, Paris

God oversees many tall building jobs
as key Architect, especially in spires
such as this; the gargoyles are affectation,
of course, Quasimodo too. But often
in His residence, the damp bleeds
from each of the interior arches
and pigeon droppings layer over time
their alabaster on the buttresses.

I climb the many medieval stairs,
twist to avoid the tourists in descent,
and am rewarded with dusty thermal inversion.

Ever (in strictly human terms) the cynic,
I will not find this city's God at any height,
nor does a father of the cloth come up
to salve unhallowed guests unsuited for eternity.

The scaffolds rise and stay; the workmen
of God arrive for their careers and camp
for a decade of genuflection for repairs;
and tourists like me walk about, caught
in the sun's reflection, snapping shots
that might reveal spirit or reverence,
flushed by heat rising in song from the holy choir.

PortugeseWave

One among continuous thousands,
the former wave rolled in
as if with unique purpose;
it spread across my feet
on the 20th of July, 1990.

In an unthinking moment, too proud,
I dumped the unfocused slide,
by what I now admit was my former self.

My journal captures what it can
but without photo documentation
I lose much of the moment.

Among a small group of world travelers,
it occurs to me that another, more distinct
image from near the same moment will do—
for, as both photo and written memory are mine,
who dares challenge the instant as unreliable?
Who dares dispute the importance of this wave?

Red Barn, Northeast Washington

That north wind punishes respect for property,
peels back sixty years of paint the hand liked –
every other year red, every year more of a tilt
toward that thin horizon stained like dried blood,
until woodwarp and nailrust urged this change
in barnshape. Warp, no wood. Rust, no nail.

Carpenters came to the barn-raising from around,
a little cranky, but loving smells of wood and needing
the barn to rise from the field, needing shelter
for stock and expensive machinery and seed.
The small community greeted carpenters.
Those living around welcomed shelter.
They painted their barns to be visible
at the ends of long years, long roads,
and bright among the long furrows.

That north wind still churns the living blood.

Round Sky with Clouds

Called range by those with senses fixed on round sky,
with clouds brushing hilltops, roads circling hillsides,
this Eastern Washington landscape fulfills my yearning.

I had dismissed it as too familiar, akin to prairie, like home
with an ache for grandeur, always falling on hard times,
often allied to the sting of its winds, carrying dust like bison
enraged when roused from a cooling roll to a heated stampede.

But now my appreciation grows, filled with clear recollection
of the day when space in the form of clouds kissed ground,
with light and me providing witness, providing Kodachrome.
No one said it would be easy to record history; no one said

there would be rewards dependent entirely on circumstance;
no one told me that I would see so much past in careless acts
of escaping the present. All along the road, the past welled up,
as though private ceremonies preceded me in the clouds,

as though my child's nightmares disappeared in ice particles,
as though nerve to engage this single angle of the universe
spun before me in dust devils, as though home waited behind
but also ahead, in the gray, in the brown, in the special green.

Skagit River, Below Diablo Dam

The devil river rests, replaced by this naked sluice
with water-worn boulders exposed to ordinary light;
a blue-green patina remains above the green, still water,
now embraced by shade: we are naked under the high dam.

I am embarrassed by another look: an ancient womb, unmoved
by the Skagit's flashing desire, exposed as though at auction
to the common light, fingers prying into nature's machinery,
as man's intellect experiments with the power of its silence.

Below, in towns, the devil's energy transmogrifies dark gestures
as bright light cheers each ruddy face turned to the corners of
night;
bright light ripples the waters that burgeon eddies in Puget Sound;
spirits rise in continuous bright lights, starting journeys to the stars.

Too, my urge toward remoteness fares no better as the waters still:
the quiet of cold forms within my mind, all but ejecting natural
heat.
I hear familiar screams, indirect, deflected by the hills, other devils
propounding mysteries, other rivers gone dry on the rocks of
desire.

I blanch at superficial analogies. I have cherished some of the
dead,
written short, successful books about death, taken leaves at sunset.
Once I picked thistles from banks of lower Skagit and tossed them
in as symbols of youth and protest. Thistles now overrun the dry
banks.

Spokane Tree

I was not drawn to Spokane for solitude.
I sought no mythical omphalos to be near.
Through the years I did my business and went home,
among thoughts of green mountains, green Seattle.

The land between augured long life, deepened endurance
while ringing the beat of lonely, dusty miles; the hands
lost touch with ordinary time, would shatter every bone,
whether wingfine or gross from the back of a captive bird.

With my spiritual sense of space, my travels made me alien,
found coping with heat, deep rain, cold, then stinging sleet,
but coping with the back edge of peace, set against the plain
like fortress walls besieged by warriors from another place.

Until one day of ennui piled on guilt prodded me to this place.
The sun prodded, too, softly showering the ground, the lake,
the tree, and its leaves with enviable, sweet light, shaking me
with tangible silence, stirring ghosts of fragile birds into flight.

Waiting for Secrets

Politics here mainly concern survival.

The grooves in the path are deep.
Someone goes over the hill regularly
and comes back as often, careful
to stay in the grooves. Tumbleweeds
depend on winds for locomotion.

The boulders in the distance
look as if from an ancient volcano
that, exploding, took the path
of least resistance, best spectacle.

It may be one hundred miles for oil
or gasoline, food and other necessities.

Probably in a pick-up, the owner
approaches the highway
as if his tires are crushing glass.

This is no country for herds.
Even chickens stay close to the house.

Both cold and heat find it suitable.
A desert encroaches, then stays.
Dark comes early and stays long.
During daylight, this place can be
its own universe; at night, it touches
directly a cataclysm of moving stars.

Photographs can last for a while;
at the time of this photograph,
the children were probably at school
to learn secrets awaited at home.

LATER

Amelia at Pacific City 1

On the gray Pacific beach, pretty Amelia feels okay:
her sweatshirt tames her friend, the owl, to ride her chest
while manly fingers, Dad's and mine, reach as tethers
for her dance between the bubbly puddles on the shore.

Amelia at Pacific City 2

Amelia's dad is Brett, who hears the waves approaching,
who knows the forlorn sea's percussion, the gray horizon,
but feels compelled to beam as though her personal sun,
and with the dusk, her personal moon and revolving star.

Blue Effulgence - 1

These windows enter into broken souls; these nails
secure asbestos siding to fresh, unsullied grooves,
to a deceiving appearance of equally unsullied tongues;
this pane waits poised like the guillotine blade over
black space, an exorbitant price for noontime shadows.

Blue Effulgence -2

Mistakes are evident. Mistakes have forced abandonment.
Yet out front at the road the fence remains closed, not locked;
the yellow grasses grow neatly—equally, as though tailored;
the sky arches in its purest blue effulgence, enticing others
to open the gate, bring a hammer, bring a saw, measure
a future night, totally committed to Orion's protection.

Buda – For or Against – Pest, 2007

Morning rose like an ice erection
in the High Tatras of Slovakia;
later a loud bus squeal and
phallic thrust of Buda into Pest.

Today we joy at left-over bridges:
we race to cover paved miles alleged,
now freed at last from socialist creed
to explore capitalist devouring by dogs.

Strung paprika, sausages, and cabbage
sting the nose as holy markets open.
Laced curtains close in hotel windows.

Sunlight races its own arc
past politics, reddens faces
and hearts conjoined in living.

At town walls, done with conjugal bone,
conjugal flesh, mourners grieve late.

Capitol Building
Salus populis suprema lex esto
Jefferson City, Missouri

Yes, ample leaves, some flowers flesh Missouri creek beds,
almost aimless; the August marble rises toward their plenty
beneath the roof; an airy wisp of cirrus cloud attends:
Jefferson himself, the champion of rural liberty,
"Let the good of the people be the supreme law."

Corinthians flute like theatre curtains before the show begins.
Lawyer legislators in summer suits rush to the state's business,
mere weeks until the primary; later all disheveled like lovers,
they disembark the sweaty ship of state to lobbyists at lunch.

The bill benefiting immigrants in the fields is tabled in committee.
And the corn, through another drought summer, turns under to
dust.

Few Cars

Behind her window she waits,
prisoner to vast space;
day after day no visitor
descends the long hill
down the road from Husavik.

Generational Ties on the Palouse

This is a local road;
the avenue for everyday movement;
the only direct access for me to local farms;
the gallery for the art of spring wheat, fall wheat
that will go gold among dispersing clouds;
and the twisting road tying the generations.

There must certainly be a road.
But I notice its minimal dimensions.
Spring shoots begin at the road's edge,
roll up to and beyond the many ridges,
while packing jauntily among their own.

There must certainly be frequent return
(for those like me unsuited to residence);
there must be bread to sustain our lives;
there must be the will to roam this road;
there must be love for local displays of light.

High on Steptoe Butte

At last, time comes round,
adores a former season
as may here be entirely consoled,
though by its turn is largely distinct.

My steady, circular climb
winds around Steptoe Butte,
again a living lace tying
never with a close touch of forever.

At the summit, my eye covets
urges in nature, remembered;
I glory; my mind sights
both green and golden wheat;
drenching light alters each kernel;
hills assent to each new swelling;
and fields push their newly realized forces.

At last, abbreviated time
splits air like the keenest knife,
dispelling cloud and doubt.

I continue within time…
with earthly permission.

Lock, Series 5560

Staunch stainless steel and brass,
utility metals, shaped in fire
for utilitarian purpose, but also
to shine in the public thoroughfare.

I cannot resist capturing a digital token.

While around me a crowd assembles
in search of the juices of fruits; the crunches
of enticing vegetables; all the hairy reds
of raspberries; the fat, lucid onion stalks;
and green, glossy sheen of sweet peppers.

There, at the corner of the city square,
weathering but resisting a persistent decay,
sits the box of power whose current brings
the visitors forth, seduces their delicious hunger,
while secure by its lock, series 5560.

Mount Rainier

If I see the mountain peak in snow,
must I know that continents adrift in time
could not avoid collision and slowly rose
to points above the trees and birds and breath?

Or, that crumbling was part of rising
from the start, that no earthly movement,
no pressure from beneath aimed at pinnacle,
no grinding heat foretold a permanent snow.

Or, if I know from my place beside a tree
that I alone can know what now I know;
that knowledge gathers at my farthest edge
if I see the mountain peak in snow?

Neighbors Passed

When the cement plant still twanged and smoked,
the boater ran the Skagit trolling for weekend fish
in the eddies off each shore, buffeting the twists
to provide for the evening barbecue, jettisoning
bones and scales to the mulch pile near the trees.

And neighbors unfailingly came by, toting white wine,
big coolers with ice and beer, potato salad by the quart:
a permanent feast laid richly on the summer's grass,
nourishing every soul with the river's shining wealth.

This craft wastes from top down now, left to endure;
frost melts in the warming day; moss drapes the rails;
mold emerged from crevices spreads its sure, languid touch.

New Light's Hard Bargain

The morning's light blazes.

My long negotiation with spirits
of rock and light, begun in dreams
spread over fading decades,
yields a peaceful legerdemain,
this magic show.

Spirits I favor posit riddles in the rocks,
wave wands of pointed light in dark recesses,
then loose more dawning to each new revelation.

Later light will require realignments, shifts of faith
along jagged, orange escarpments,
sure-footed and nimble at its edges;
later light will contain my memories.

Fitful sleep shown with doubt, fierce suspicions
much like demigods twirling on slippery ice,
distant from me and my turgid humanity,
yet auguring a bloody light wedded to stone,
presentiments untouched by day's realities.

There was a time, like this time,
when sand settled to the bottom of the sea,
grave but untroubled by any magic.
But its face is here, red-eyed, austere,
breaking into mineral effusions,
revealing more of its own elements,
more indifference to deciphering,
ready for carvings, ready for illusions.

Nor Iron, Nor Rock, Nor Gold

Three trees at the mall, with ample room for growth,
still too slim even to hint at girth displacing 25 rings
of iron, hundreds of years of mall survival, 10 to 15
generations passing with Nordstrom totes, fashions
of new materials, new designs, glamorous styles, sexy
or sedate, sensuous curves, scarf-enveloped, air-propelled.

Sap, leaves, and gum will stain the concrete sidewalk, requiring
thousands of cleanings by ever-changing maintenance crews;
kids will mature, abandon families mid-shop, likely not
to think again of the trees, the iron expansion rings, the market
for polyesters, or the local politics that shield exchange, taxes
to revitalize the long-enduring infrastructure, even the family
names.

When I give serious consideration to the future, I do not gauge it
by any kind of bands, nor iron, nor rock, nor gold in a wedding
ring:
instead I count not storekeepers but statesmen, not athletes or
games
but attitudes shaping spheres of influence; judgments by those
who earn the right to judge, while judging, guide a worthy people
to forge expanding rights, to free their minds to service justice.

Orange Fog in Pursuit Up H Street

From my driveway, after eleven years in remote hills,
for the first time I witness the assertion of orange fog.

The coming pick-up may escape an elemental absorption;
the shivering road's markings stand by, cannot contain it;
the trees stand purely, greenly amazed as nature's seed
engulfs the valley, shooting forth light along the wires,
bent on reclamation of land, air, and watery orange glow.

Spite the Obvious

At last, fruitful April of showers tempts again with performance,
aligns us at this edge, to kneel to this ocean of believable red,
to consider disbelief in flower deities a grievous fraud, a lie
cartoonish in its spite of what is obvious, what is surely true.

A tulip phalanx, pastel shields drawn, green spears ranked
across the battle field, ongoing clones soldiering to triumph;
beauty finally lost to distinction, fully obedient to superior will;
pawns to the chessman, fodder to cannon and tiller, glory to sun
for a moment, soil enrichers for the next when its bow perfects.

The Man on the Bremerton Ferry

All I miss adds volume to time's vacuum.
Solitude evokes from me a feeble say.

Random events may:
check a need for friends;
misdirect a stroll to a run for one's life;
strengthen resolve to rebuild from unmet conditions;
surround me with fruitful space; fail me silently;
course cosmic lives to intersect on ferries;
give voice an object, with time ever running on.

So, I am ready today for this man who talks
at me as though long absent, well-met, avuncular;
as though the ferry lounge were his parlor;
as though the red-satin sunset his personal illumination;
and I his shy, intimate relative or friend, chosen
to register in script his painful tales
and collaborate in the loss of his faculties
before dark and wet weather settle in.

Although on my way I am not his friend,
I am where he needs his friend to be.

With his smile, he creates convenience.

His eyes, so weakened, obscure justice.
I am contrite for whatever is my guilt.

And on we go until my silence fills me
like a basin with showers overflowing.

With his voice always more at ease,
I steal another's life,
my felony an act of uneasy will.

I shake in his reverend air. His blessing offers
ample commutation to fit an hour trip.

His frankness frightens me. I am more shy.

On other occasions, in its glide
through Puget Sound, the *Yakima*
has calmed my eddy in its wake,
has excited fervor for this land of waters.

Not this time.

When finally I talk, my words inherit voices:
a stupid man who mumbles an inane
homage to dinner and freedom;
the cornered man, agreeable to a fault,
anxious for his own release; and
a man who shares his heart,
as at home, or in the parlor of a friend,
freely at ease with age, with hurt,
and generous with empathy.

When he departs the vessel, the man
on the Bremerton ferry,
I am changed, liberated
to afford a last assumption:
warm at home, he relaxes in his chair,
grateful having met his old friend
at a moment of calm
before the evening storm.

Returning to Seattle,
I am grateful for his error
and envy his friendships.

Washington State Route 20
North Cascades National Park

Another week will close the highway and pass,
causing me to wonder about conditioning to hike
the mountain trails to lakes always denied me now.

I settle for what the open road fulfills, sedentary
at the wheel, willing enough to document a light
lolling among the drooping grasses, venerating
the fallen logs that floated here and lodged in ice,
and the deep blue of a roadside pool unnoticed
by every other passerby, bound to arid Winthrop
or electric generators gunning at Newhalem.

Crater Without Device

I cannot approach beyond road's end. I am no explorer.
Remaining mountain snow tempers even this timid approach.
How can I know the crater without perspective on it?
Strong contrariness, like a harness, holds me rapt, here.

My photo exaggerates the rim's trembling at the sky,
courtesy of my polarizing filter: dense blue saturates.

I've captured light at its moment of formulation,
clarity exempt from space's interference, begetter
of unnatural beauty's eruption in high resolution.

Yet, I find from a safe perspective, I can go farther:
a crater appears without device, preternaturally,
with no eruptions of subterranean gases, silently;
already dormant, quiet but for punishing winds,
circling and plunging well above absolute tree line,
with no more need as foundation than presence of light.

No Argument Rises

Iron-tinged landscape layers in insistence,
as if forced by heat to say, "choose me."
I am rarely caught unresponsive, asleep,
gasping in the smeared red, even longing
for the cool blue rising in the background.

These rocks have been possessed by natural men,
pony-men always looking for, always finding
sun lighting their war. I cannot pioneer, I can
roar an echo over abandonment, or sit dejected
by the gila's shape alive in an adopted hole.

"Valley of Fire?" No sane argument rises on wind,
no sere lip, raging blood, or bubbled eye objects;
and all the bones (see the knees and elbows rising
from the sand?) eschew their tissue for mute stones.

www.ingramcontent.com/pod-product-compliance
Lightning Source LLC
Chambersburg PA
CBHW042337150426
43195CB00001B/24